THE JOSHUA MINISTRY

"GOD'S WITNESSING ARMY"

A systematic evangelism
strategy based in principle on
the Book of Joshua

Evangelism Implementation Manual

David Hopewell, Sr., D.Min.

The Joshua Ministry
Evangelism Implementation Manual

by
David Hopewell, Sr., D.Min.

ISBN 0-9786056-0-8

Published by The Joshua Ministry
1772 Enid Drive
Lithonia, GA 30058

Book design by Faith Instructional Design, Inc.

Table of Contents

The Joshua Ministry Model

Introduction

The Joshua Ministry is an evangelism strategy that mobilizes the body of Christ to go into their communities and help their lost brothers and sisters take back what Satan has stolen from them. This strategy may be used by any church of any denomination to kindle a passion for unsaved people in their congregations and to systematically share the gospel of Jesus Christ in their communities.

This manual provides step-by-step procedures on implementing the Joshua Ministry strategy in your local church. A complete description of the strategy and its underlying principles is available in *The Joshua Ministry: God's Witnessing Army* by Rev. David Hopewell, Sr.

Topics

This chapter contains the following topics:

Topic	Page
Overview	2
Principles for Successful Evangelism	6

Overview

Foundation

The Joshua Ministry is based on biblical principles from the Book of Joshua. As the Israelites where preparing to enter the Promised Land, Joshua called together the tribes of Reuben, Gad and Manasseh and reminded them of the commission Moses had given to "help your brothers possess their land."

> But to the Reubenites, the Gadites and the half-tribe of Manasseh, Joshua said, "Remember the command that Moses the servant of the LORD gave you: 'The LORD your God is giving you rest and has granted you this land.' Your wives, your children and your livestock may stay in the land that Moses gave you east of the Jordan, but all your fighting men, fully armed, must cross over ahead of your brothers. You are to help your brothers until the LORD gives them rest, as he has done or you, and until they too have taken possession of the land that the LORD your God is giving them. After that, you may go back and occupy your own land, which Moses the servant of the LORD gave you east of the Jordan toward the sunrise" (Joshua 1:12–15).

Just as Joshua reminded the Israelites to cross the Jordan to help their brothers possess their land, we, too, must cross over any obstacle to help our brothers and sisters evangelize their neighborhoods and meet the needs of others until their communities are possessed by God.

Vision

The Joshua Ministry has a two-fold vision. First, Sunday School (Fulfillment Hour) classes help their class members evangelize (possess their land) in their neighborhoods. Secondly, churches within the same zip code, town or city come together helping each other (possess their land) through evangelizing and meeting the needs of residents through church ministries, para-church ministries, or existing organizations.

The vision calls for members of the body of Christ to go door by door, and street by street until the entire land is possessed. The goal is to fulfill the Great Commission in Matthew 28 by moving congregants from sitting in the pews to a lifestyle of active evangelism.

How It Works
The Joshua Ministry does not replace your existing evangelism ministry. Instead, it provides a systematic strategy to bring consistency to your evangelism efforts. Your Evangelism Ministry uses the Joshua Ministry strategies to partner with other ministries of the church and engage as many people as possible in regularly scheduled intentional evangelism activities. The Joshua Ministry equips congregations to effectively communicate the gospel and holistically minister to their neighbors using four major strategies:

Members Helping Members
The adult Sunday School classes are grouped into tribes just as in Joshua 1:12–15. Members in the class identify neighborhoods or individuals they wish to evangelize. The class or tribe goes door-to-door together, meeting the natural needs of the people in the community and sharing the gospel.

Churches Helping Churches
Like the tribes in Joshua 1, churches work together to help each other possess the land. In the unity of faith, churches come together, divide the targeted neighborhood, and then go door-to-door, street by street and block by block, sharing Christ and meeting needs until the entire area is reached.

"The Joshua Generation: God's Witnessing Army"
The Joshua Generation are the young people society has labeled Generation X. These young people are powerful instruments of God and can make a difference in the lives of their peers. Their excitement and concern motivates our youth to minister to others.

Special Forces
Just as Joshua had a special group to go spy out the land, the Special Forces team helps pastors plant new churches. The Special Forces evangelize at night in places where Satan has the greatest influence, e.g., liquor stores and night clubs. The people in these places are hurting and lost. Most are filled with hopelessness and despair. The Special Forces are trained to reach out to these people and help them break free from Satan's grip.

Specific tactics for these strategies are described in the chapter entitled Witnessing Tactics. The Joshua Ministry uses these strategies to create a system through which the entire church is mobilized to:

- Consistently and intentionally share the gospel
- Meet the needs of people in their community
- Help new converts begin a life of discipleship

Overview (con'td)

Organizational Structure

The Joshua Ministry is designed to be implemented primarily through the Sunday School in partnership with the Prayer Ministry. However, it may also be implemented through any ministry that wants to be involved in intentional evangelism.

Evangelism Ministry

Role

Provide vision, training and leadership

Positions

Minister of Evangelism
Tribal Leaders
Training Team
Demographics Team
Communication Team
Follow-Up Team

Prayer Ministry

Role

Provide leadership and training
in intercession

Positions

Intercessors

Sunday School or Other Ministries

Role

Provide people to go out and witness

Positions

Outreach Leader
Prayer Leader
Assimilation Leader

Overview (con'td)

How It Began

God birthed the Joshua Ministry in the heart of Rev. David W. Hopewell, Sr. in 1997. The strategy was first implemented at Greenforest Community Baptist Church in Decatur Georgia where Rev. Hopewell is the Minister of Evangelism. Since then he has assisted churches throughout the United States in using the Joshua Ministry as their evangelism strategy. Because of the Joshua Ministry, the gospel has been shared with thousands and many have accepted Jesus as their personal Savior.

Greenforest uses a non-traditional Sunday School model called Fulfillment Hour. Fulfillment Hour fulfills the five-fold purpose of the church—evangelism, discipleship, worship, fellowship and ministry/missions—through small groups.

Each Fulfillment Hour class has nine positional leaders who lead their class members in fulfilling God's purposes. Those that directly support the Joshua Ministry are:

- **Outreach Leader** —Leads the class members in evangelism by encouraging class members to participate in regularly scheduled evangelism blitzes and requesting the class' assistance in evangelizing their neighborhoods, family members and friends,
- **Prayer Leader** – Leads class members in developing their personal prayer lives and joins with other Prayer Leaders to intercede for all evangelism activities
- **Assimilation Leader** – Helps new converts become a part of the church family and Fulfillment Hour class

Greenforest's adult Fulfillment Hour classes are divided into four tribes: Reuben, Gad, Manasseh and Ephraim. The tribes participate in regularly scheduled evangelism visitations.

You will see references to Fulfillment Hour throughout this manual. If you would like to learn more about the model, I encourage you to read *Fulfillment Hour*, by Jackie S. Henderson and Joan W. Johnson. This book provides a complete description of the Fulfillment Hour model and instructions for implementing it in any local church.

Principles for Successful Evangelism

Introduction

The Book of Joshua provides several principles that guarantee a successful evangelism effort. When practiced consistently, these principles will overcome the evil one and prepare the hearts of the people in the targeted area for a plentiful harvest.

Spy the Land

"And Joshua the son of Nun sent out of Shittim two men to spy secretly, saying, Go view the land, even Jericho" (Joshua 2:1).

To "spy the land" means becoming aware of the demographics of the neighborhood. This includes the residents, their needs and the problems that plague the neighborhood. It also includes identifying other ministries and faith-based organizations within the community that can help bring solutions.

Follow God's Direction

"And they commanded the people, saying, When ye see the ark of the covenant of the LORD your God, and the priest the Levites bearing it, then ye shall remove from your place, and go after it…for you have not passed this way heretofore" (Joshua 3:3–4).

God gave specific direction throughout the Book of Joshua as to how the Israelites were to possess the land. God may have a specific strategy to take the land and meet the needs of the community. I have found that God will lead you to the right person, who is receptive and has a real need for ministry at a specific time. If we are not directed by God, we can miss the move of God.

Sanctify Yourself

"And Joshua said unto the people, Sanctify yourselves for tomorrow the LORD will do wonders among you" (Joshua 3:5).

To "sanctify" means to be set apart or set aside for God's service. It is a commitment to be sensitive to God's leading. It means that we allow God and His gifts to flow through us. This commitment must start with cleansing ourselves of any known sin in our lives. God will not be present in the battle if there is sin in the camp. When we sanctify ourselves, God will dwell with us and fight our battles for us.

Move Out on Faith

"And it shall come to pass, as soon as the soles of the feet of the priests that bear the ark of the LORD, the Lord of all the earth, shall rest in the waters of Jordan, that the waters of Jordan shall be cut off from the waters that come down from above; and they shall stand upon an heap. And it came to pass as the people remove from their tents to pass over Jordan and the priest bearing the ark of the covenant before the people" (Joshua 3:13–14).

There must always must be an element of faith. As long as the task seems overwhelming, the glory will be God's alone. When we realize our inability to accomplish what God has told us to do, we depend on His help. The Israelites stepped out on faith as God led the way. We must first move out on faith before God will manifest His power in our efforts.

God Will Confirm His Presence

"And Joshua said, Hereby ye shall know that the living God is among you, and that he will without fail drive out from before you the Canaanites, and the Hittites, and the…" (Joshua 3:10).

As long as the Israelites sanctified themselves and faith was present, God showed up and showed out. We will know God is with us when lives are changed. We will also hear comments from those to whom we are witnessing, confirming our divine appointments, e.g., "I was just praying for God to send help."

God Will Give You a Testimony

"That this may be a sign among you, that when your children ask their fathers in time to come, saying, What mean ye by these stones? Then ye shall answer them" (Joshua 4:6–7).

If we cleanse ourselves and move out in obedience, God will always do miraculous things we can share with others as a testimony of His presence and power. These testimonies will generate excitement for your ministry and lead others to Christ.

Continue the Campaign

"And the priests that bare the ark of the covenant of the LORD stood firm on dry ground in the midst of Jordan, and all the Israelites passed over on dry ground, until all the people were passed clean over Jordan" (Joshua 3:17).

In Joshua 3:11–17, when the priests put their feet in the water, the Jordan River divided. When we get involved in people's lives and communities, we must continue our efforts. If not, their lives will return to their original state just as the waters went back together when the priests removed their feet from the Jordan. Our evangelism efforts must be a continuous campaign.

Give God the Glory

"Then Joshua built an altar unto the LORD God of Israel in mount Ebal" *(Joshua 8:30).*

After victory at Ai, Joshua built an altar to the Lord who gave them the victory. We must never be guilty of stealing the glory that only belongs to God. We cannot take credit for what He does in our midst. Be careful to praise only Him.

Implementation Process

Introduction

This chapter describes the steps you should follow to implement the Joshua Ministry strategy in your church. Each phase of the process is described with its:

- Purpose
- Milestone events
- Result

Topics

This chapter contains the following topics:

Implementation Overview

Introduction   These are the steps required to implement the Joshua Ministry in your church. Each step will be explained in greater detail on the subsequent pages.

Pastor Orientation

Gain the pastor's agreement and support to implement the Joshua Ministry.

▼

Leadership Orientation

Communicate evangelism vision to the church's leadership.

▼

Vision Communication

Communicate God's vision for the church to the congregation.

▼

Prayer, Praise and Worship

Cover the church and community with prayer and the Holy Spirit.

Implementation Overview (cont'd)

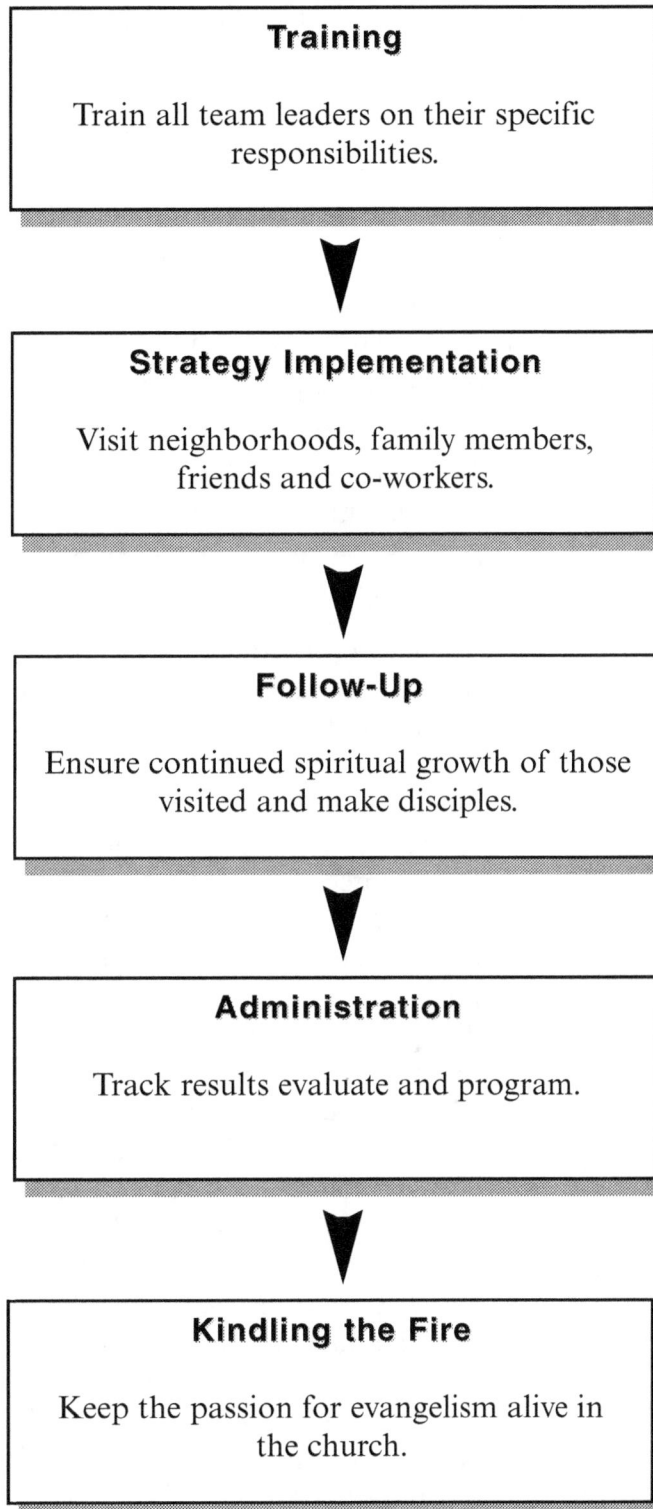

Training

Train all team leaders on their specific responsibilities.

▼

Strategy Implementation

Visit neighborhoods, family members, friends and co-workers.

▼

Follow-Up

Ensure continued spiritual growth of those visited and make disciples.

▼

Administration

Track results evaluate and program.

▼

Kindling the Fire

Keep the passion for evangelism alive in the church.

Pastor Orientation

Purpose

The purpose of the Pastor Orientation is to gain the pastor's agreement and support to implement the Joshua Ministry strategy.

Many of you reading this book are pastors who are looking for a biblically-based strategy to build your evangelism ministry. That is wonderful! I congratulate you on taking a leadership role in moving your congregation from the pews into the harvest fields. It does not matter if you are a senior pastor, associate pastor or a lay leader, leadership begins at the top. The pastor must see the Joshua Ministry as part of God's provision for the church's vision. Once the pastor discerns that the Joshua Ministry is part of God's will for your church, then he or she must commit to actively support the evangelism ministry with leadership and resources. The Joshua Ministry cannot be successfully implemented without the pastor's complete support.

Milestone Event

The Minister of Evangelism meets with the pastor to discuss the following:

- The church needs to evangelize. God wants His church to keep the first thing first. Jesus came to set the captives free. His mission is still our mission today.
- There are people in your community who are lost, headed to hell and no one cares.
- There are people in your community with needs that are going unmet. God has planted your church in its specific community to meet the holistic needs of the people living there.
- It is not necessary for the pastor to bear the load of the church's five-fold purpose alone. God created the church for the purpose of evangelism, discipleship, fellowship, worship ministry/missions. It is not necessary for the pastor to fulfill these purposes alone. Ephesians 4:8–12 tells us that when Christ ascended to heaven, He gave gifts to all men (and women) for the perfecting of the saints and the edifying of the Body of Christ. "And he gave some, apostles; and some, prophets; and some, evangelists; and some, pastors and teachers" (Ephesians 4:11). God has placed others in the body to help carry out ministry. Utilizing the gifts of those God has placed within your congregation will release the power of the Holy Spirit in your church and cause it to thrive.
- In order to successfully implement the Joshua Ministry strategy, the pastor must have a teachable spirit and be willing empower others to lead.
- Keeping the fire of evangelism alive in the church requires a continuous promotion of evangelism from the pulpit. Will the pastor commit to promoting evangelism from the pulpit on an ongoing basis?
- What resources can the church allocate to this evangelism effort?

Pastor Orientation (cont'd)

Result

The Pastor Orientation enables the pastor to:

- Understand the biblical foundation of the Joshua Ministry and, hopefully, recognize it as a movement of God.
- Go before God to discern if the Joshua Ministry is within God's will for your church at this time.
- Actively support implementation of the Joshua Ministry in your local church, if directed by God .
- Answer questions regarding the Joshua Ministry with confidence and boldness based on God's Word.
- Partner with the Minister of Evangelism and others to lead the church in winning souls for Christ.

Leadership Orientation

Purpose

The purpose of the Leadership Orientation is to gain agreement and support from the church leadership to implement the Joshua Ministry strategy.

Milestone Event

The Evangelism Ministry meets with the church leadership to:

- Communicate the evangelism vision to the church leadership.
- Describe the Joshua Ministry strategy.
- Answer any questions.
- Introduce key leaders and their responsibilities.
- Solicit help and suggestions from other leaders.

Result

The church leadership and Evangelism Ministry are on one accord and both clearly understand:

- God's mandate for your church.
- The vision.
- The strategy.
- Resources needed to support the ministry.

Planning the Meeting

The success of your meeting depends on prayer and preparation. Pray for God to help you discern how to present the Joshua Ministry information so it will be received well by the church's leadership. Take the following steps to prepare for the meeting:

- Develop vision and mission statements for your evangelism ministry. Your vision statement should describe what your ministry hopes to ultimately accomplish. Another way of describing your vision is how the world will be different because of your existence. Your mission statement describes what you do now to accomplish your future vision.
- List objectives. Make sure they are measurable so you will know when you have accomplished them.
- Select the Joshua Ministry strategies and tactics you will implement. (See Strategy Implementation and Witnessing Tactics for details.)
- Determine what resources are needed. Be sure to include people, materials and facilities.
- Reserve the room.
- Arrange for audio/visual equipment, if needed.

Vision Communication

Purpose

The purpose of this phase is to communicate God's vision for the church to the congregation and to gain their support in carrying out the Joshua Ministry strategy.

Milestone Events

Communication of the vision occurs over one month. The following events take place during that time:

- Describe the vision and Joshua strategy to the congregation and Sunday School (Fulfillment Hour).
- Emphasize evangelism for one month in sermons, Sunday School (Fulfillment Hour) lessons, and Bible study.
- Provide witnessing training during Sunday School (Fulfillment Hour) classes as well as weekly Saturday classes. See the Training section for more information.

Result

The congregation and Sunday School (Fulfillment Hour) members clearly understand:

- God's vision for the church as related to evangelism.
- What God's expects from every believer regarding evangelism and missions according to Matthew 28:19–21.
- Their personal call to evangelism and missions in their Jerusalem, Judea, Samaria, or to the uttermost parts of the earth.
- The Joshua Ministry strategy and how it will be implemented.

Information to Provide

In addition to the vision, your message should clarify how your congregation becomes involved in the Joshua Ministry by providing:

- Training times and locations.
- Brief descriptions of the leadership positions, e.g., tribal leaders, prayer leaders, assimilation leaders. etc.
- Instructions to register for leadership positions and training.
- Suggestions for how other ministries in can partner with the evangelism ministry and who to contact.

Prayer, Praise and Worship

Purpose

The purpose of the prayer phase is to employ the entire congregation. Before we begin evangelizing, we must pray, praise and worship to:

- Break the chains of fear, apathy and rebellion that hold church members in their pews.
- Prick the hearts of your congregation so they will have compassion for people who are hurting and lost.
- Break down walls of resistance among those to whom you will witness and replace them with receptive hearts.
- Enlist the power of the Holy Spirit to lead, direct, speak, convict and draw the lost.

Milestone Event

The Evangelism Ministry, Prayer Ministry and Sunday School (Fulfillment Hour) Prayer Leaders cover the entire process with prayer. They pray for:

- Church members who are chained to the pews.
- The lost who do not know Christ.
- The atmosphere of the community and the demolition of territorial spirits.

Result

Through prayer and the working of the Holy Spirit:

- The church will be on one accord.
- God will release a spirit of evangelism in the church.
- God will raise up laborers to go into the mission field.
- The eyes of the congregation will be opened to the power that is available to them through the Holy Spirit.
- Doors will be opened to witness and ministry.
- Yokes will be broken over the lives of family members, loved ones, co-workers, neighbors, and friends.
- People will repent, believe and accept Jesus as their Savior.

The Importance of Prayer

We need to use prayer, praise and worship as weapons to break down walls of resistance. In Joshua 6, the shout of praise brought down the walls of Jericho. We must first develop our personal prayer life. Then, we can effectively pray for the lost. Out of a consistent fervent prayer life, one becomes committed and can then say, "Not my will Lord, but thy will be done."

Through prayer, we become more sensitive to the lost, and ascertain God's heart of concern for them. Through prayer, a passion for the hurting and lost will surface in our lives. We cannot spend time with God and not feel what He feels or see what He sees; nor can we not respond to it. When we do not feel compassion in our hearts for those who hurt or are lost, it clearly indicates we are not spending much time in prayer.

Prayer, Praise and Worship (cont'd)

The Importance of Prayer (cont'd)	Evangelism without prayer only results in a stubborn will and a hard heart in those whom we try to reach. In Joshua 3:3 and11, the people did not move unless the Ark of the Covenant, symbolizing God's presence, went before them. Likewise, we must have God's presence go ahead of us to assure victory. Like David, we should ask the Lord in what direction does He want us to go. David wanted God to go before him. If God was not going before him, he knew he could not prevail in battle (I Samuel 30). Without prayer, we will find ourselves engaged in demonic activity that could have been held back through our efforts in prayer.
Praying for Church Members	When praying for the members of your church, pray: ■ That God releases a spirit of evangelism in the church. In Acts 1:8, when the Holy Spirit fell on them, He brought a spirit of evangelism to reach beyond Jerusalem. ■ Against the powers of darkness and the spirits of apathy, unbelief and rebellion that hold us in our pews (Daniel 10:13, Ephesians 6). ■ That God raises up laborers to go into the mission field (Matthew 9:37, 38). Jesus said that the fields were white all ready to harvest, but the laborers were few (John 4:35). Ask God to raise up church members who will answer the call to share Christ with a dying world. Jesus said that we should pray to the Lord of Harvest to raise labors to gather the harvest (Matthew 9:38). ■ For eyes to be opened to God's calling, our inheritance and the power that is available to us, which is the same power that raised Christ from the dead. Ephesians 1:18–20 specifically teaches us what we should pray for our fellow believers.
Praying for the Lost	When we pray for the lost, we must pray: ■ For territorial spirits are demolished. ■ That the Heavenly Father draws the lost (John 6:44). Only God can draw men to Himself. ■ Against spiritual blindness (Ephesians 1:18–20; 2 Corinthians 4:3,4). Although Paul was writing to believers, there is a principle that applies to the lost as well. We can pray that the eyes of the lost be open so they may know what the hope of God's calling is for them. ■ That the Holy Spirit convicts lost persons (John 16:8). A man will never see his sin, unless the Holy Spirit reveals it to him. The Holy Spirit has to bring conviction of the sin in one's life.

Prayer, Praise and Worship (cont'd)

Praying for the Lost (cont'd)

- For receptive hearts (Luke 8:5, 12); a lost person's heart needs to be broken to receive the seed of the gospel. Mark 4 reveals different types of ground. The reception of the seed is based on the soil, which represents the heart. If the heart is hard, the soil is hard. If the heart is soft, the soil is fertile ground and can receive the seed of God's Word. We need to pray for God to give the lost person a receptive heart.
- That God grants repentance to unbelievers (II Timothy 2:25). God's goodness leads men to repent (Romans 2:4).

We should make intercessory prayer or stand in the gap for the lost (I Timothy 2:1–3). When we intercede, we plead on their behalf before God. We have to remember that most unbelievers feel dirty, ashamed and unworthy. They feel they cannot come to God. We know God wants them to come to Him and repent, but Satan has blinded their minds. Through prayer, we stand in their place and bring them into the presence of God. We should ask God to open their eyes to see Him and not the church. If they look at the church, Satan will gladly show them the faults.

Prayer Strategy

The Evangelism Ministry partners with the Prayer Ministry to implement the following prayer strategy. If your church does not have a Prayer Ministry, then organize a group of members who have the gift of intercession.

Follow these steps to initiate a prayer strategy:

Step	Action
1	Train all Evangelism and Prayer Ministry Leaders how to pray effectively over the target area and its residents. If the church is using the Fulfillment Hour model, include the Prayer Leaders from the Fulfillment Hour classes.
2	Enlist other Sunday School (Fulfillment Hour) class members to pray along with you.
3	Get a map of the targeted area from Demographic Team and/or names of family members, co-workers, friends, and neighbors and begin to pray over them and fast to break strongholds in their life.
4	If they receive Christ, pray that Christ be formed in them (Galatians 4:19).
5	Pray for any needs that they may have.

NOTE: The Prayer Ministry may consider a prayer walk in the targeted area.

Training

Purpose	During the training phase, all Joshua Ministry leaders are trained on their specific responsibilities and duties.
Milestone Events	Separate training sessions are conducted with each of the following Joshua Ministry leadership teams:

- Demographics Team
- Tribal Leaders
- Outreach Leaders
- Prayer Leaders and Intercessors
- Communication Team
- Follow-Up Team
- Assimilation Leaders

NOTE: See the Training section for details on training each position. I recommend limiting each session to no more than a half day (four hours). Be sure to schedule at least two sessions for each position on varying days and times to accommodate different work schedules.

Result

All leaders will know:

- Their responsibilities.
- How to effectively accomplish their tasks.
- The interdependencies between the members of each team.

Planning Training

Follow these steps when planning your training:

Step	Action
1	Ask the Communication Team to help recruit workers for all leadership positions.
2	Encourage other ministries to consider how they can partner with the Evangelism Ministry to reach the lost and include their outreach leaders in the training.
3	Reserve the room, audio/visual equipment and arrange for refreshments.
4	Obtain sufficient copies of all training materials, including forms, tracts, etc.

Strategy Implementation

Purpose

The purpose of this phase is to share the gospel with neighbors, family, friends and co-workers. The Joshua Ministry strategy is a church-wide effort to reach the lost via the Sunday School (Fulfillment Hour) and personal evangelism. Many tactics may be used. Be creative. There is no limit to what God can do.

Milestone Events

The Joshua Ministry uses four major strategies to reach the lost:

- Members Helping Members
- Churches Helping Churches
- The Joshua Generation: God's Witnessing Army (Youth)
- Special Forces

These strategies are carried out using mass evangelism and personal evangelism tactics. Many of the tactics can be used to support multiple strategies. The following is a list of tactics that may be used for each strategy. See Witnessing Tactics for specific instructions for each tactic.

Members Helping Members

Guest Cards
Multiplication By One
Seed Casting
Set the Captives Free
Tract Distribution

Churches Helping Churches

Adopt-a-Neighborhood
Blitz
Crusade
Neighborhood Projects
Seed Casting
Tract Distribution

Strategy Implementation (cont'd)

Milestone Events (cont'd)

Joshua Generation: God's Witnessing Army

Brother-to-Brother
Guest Cards
Set the Captives Free
Tract Distribution

Special Forces

Blitz
Guest Cards
Tract Distribution

Here is another way of looking at these tactics:

Personal Evangelism

Guest Cards
Multiplication by One
Set the Captives Free
Tract Distribution

Mass Evangelism

Adopt-a-Neighborhood
Blitz
Brother-to-Brother
Crusade
Guest Cards
Neighborhood Projects
Seed Casting
Set the Captives Free
Tract Distribution

Result

Visitations, prayer and concern for those visited will result in:

- The love of Christ being demonstrated to non-Christians.
- People in your community being ministered to and their needs being met.
- Members leaving the pews and going behind enemy lines to minister to those held in the captivity of sin.
- The gospel being shared with the lost.
- Non-members visiting the church.
- Sunday School (Fulfillment Hour) enrollment increasing.
- Worship and Sunday School (Fulfillment Hour) attendance increasing.
- God's kingdom growing.

Follow-Up

Purpose

The purpose of the follow-up phase is to:

- Ensure the continued spiritual growth and well being of those visited.
- Assimilate new converts into the family of God.
- Make disciples who will make other disciples.

Milestone Events

Follow-up is the responsibility of every church member who participates in the evangelism activities. Members are expected to:

- Contact the people they talked to during the visitations, especially those who prayed to receive Christ.
- Help meet any immediate needs by securing resources or referring the person to the appropriate ministry within the church, a para-church organization or governmental agency.
- Invite the people to whom they witnessed to church.
- Help them contact another churchIf they are not interested in your church.
- Encourage the new converts in their spiritual growth.
- Teach them to witness. Invite them to attend a Soul-Winning Evangelism Workshop, and go with them.
- Go with them to share Christ, and model the process for them.

The Joshua Ministry Follow-Up Team will coordinate with the Sunday School (Fulfillment Hour) teachers/shepherds to confirm that follow-up is taking place and to provide assistance in meeting the needs of those to whom the church has witnessed.

Result

By following up:

- People's needs will be met.
- The church will actually be the hands and feet of Jesus in the community.
- New converts will form discipling relationships to support their spiritual growth.
- The church will grow, spiritually and numerically.

Assimilating New Converts

Four important messages should be communicated to converts immediately:

- "You have a whole new family that is anxiously waiting to meet you."
- "I know you want to grow in your relationship with God. I suggest reading the Book of John because it will help you understand who Jesus is through His life and His works."
- "I know you pray. Now that you have been reborn, you will want to spend more time in prayer, communing with God."
- "God has given you the precious gift of eternal life. It is too good to keep to yourself. Let me teach you how to share this gift with others."

Follow-Up (cont'd)

Making Disciples

Making converts alone is not fulfilling the Great Commission! Jesus' command was to make disciples, not converts. Only healthy disciples reproduce. The success of the Great Commission depends on multiplication. If we (the church) fail to make disciples, it fails.

We must produce new disciples who will make more disciples. Everyone who learns to share the gospel, must mentor another to do the same. See Multiplication By One under Witnessing Tactics for instructions on discipling others.

There are three things you should do to teach new converts how to witness:

Step	Action
1	Invite new converts to the Soul-Winning Evangelism Workshop and go with them.
2	Invite them to join you on visitations and let them see you model the process of sharing Christ.
3	Share the following do's and don'ts of visitations: ■ Don't pressure people. ■ Do be kind, caring, and demonstrate the love of Christ. ■ Do respect people's time, circumstances and decision. NOTE: See the Soul-Winning Evangelism Workshop for instructions on visitations.
4	Go with them on their first visitation.

Tracking Results

Purpose

The purpose of recording your results is to honor God for the work of His Holy Spirit and to get your congregants excited about what God is doing through your church. Keeping track of results will help you:

- Recognize the powerful work of God and enable you to thank Him for the victory.
- Know how many lives are being affected by your efforts.
- Identify where adjustments should be made to increase your effectiveness.
- Plan and project resource needs

Milestone Events

Record the results of each evangelism event and report them to the church. I recommend having a weekly evangelism report in your Sunday bulletin. It is particularly effective for the pastor to announce this information from the pulpit each Sunday.

For each event, record the number of people:

- From your church who participated (first timers and total attendance)
- With whom you shared Christ
- Who received Christ
- Who rededicated their lives to Christ
- With whom you prayed for their needs
- Who enrolled in Sunday School (Fulfillment Hour)

NOTE: See Administrative Forms for examples of reports.

Kindling the Fire

Purpose

Unfortunately, the new fire for evangelism may burn out if it is not constantly tended. "Kindling the Fire" is an ongoing effort to keep the church's passion for the lost alive.

Milestone Events

Make a deliberate, ongoing effort to keep the fire alive by:

- **Pray.** A weakening fire is evidence of a weak prayer. Keep a strong prayer life, corporately and individually.
- **Lead by example.** Leadership sets the tone. Lead your troops into battle, and they will follow.
- **Change your fishing spot (Luke 5:1–7).** If the fish are not biting, change where you fish. Little or no response may indicate it is time to evangelize elsewhere.
- **Provide opportunities for engagement.** Always create the place and environment for evangelism. Make sure there is always an active tactic for "intentional evangelism" to purposely go out and witness.
- **Testify.** Share testimonies about your evangelism efforts in the congregation. This will ignite others in the congregation to join the cause.

Result

Your church will be continuously filled with compassion for the lost and the power to witness. God will save many through your efforts and your church will be blessed.

Leadership Training

Introduction

This chapter contains training information for leaders in the Evangelism, Prayer and Sunday School (Fulfillment Hour) ministries who will be involved in carrying out the Joshua Ministry Strategy.

Topics

This chapter contains the following topics:

The Benefit of Effective Training

If we would be honest, there are a number of churches that hold evangelism seminars, but after the seminar is over, the spirit of evangelism begins to die. Teaching and preaching for the most part takes place in the sanctuary, or in a classroom setting. However, my experience has shown that to have an effective ongoing evangelism ministry, training must always be a part of the equation.

Training takes place in the field and guarantees the existence of the evangelism ministry beyond the teaching seminar. If we have a seminar without providing an opportunity to practice what was taught, the excitement will only last as long as the seminar. The workshop becomes just another evangelism seminar the members attended. This problem occurs because what was learned was not implemented. Consequently, the spirit of evangelism dies.

Knowledge that is not acted upon will only leave people in bondage. Jesus said, *"And ye shall know the truth, and the truth shall make you free" (John 8:32).* He was saying truth liberates. When we act on God's Word and press past the fear that chains us to our pews, then we will be free.

Tremendous benefits are reaped when we take what we learned in the classroom to the field (neighborhoods). How rewarding it is to be used by God to change someone's life; to be God's ears that hear, His voice that speaks, or His hand that touches. These benefits can only be experienced as we move from the pew to the streets and begin to witness to others. The benefits of leaving the classroom and taking what we have learned to the streets are literally life changing. It will:

- Break comfort zones.
- Destroy fear.
- Activate faith.
- Encourage others.
- Produce a testimony.
- Give experience.
- Open a door for spiritual gifts.

Preparing to Train

When planning your training:

- Ask the Communication Team to help recruit workers.
- Encourage other ministries to consider how they can partner with the Evangelism Ministry to reach the lost.
- Schedule multiple training sessions for each position at different times to make it convenient for various work schedules.
- Reserve the room, audio/visual equipment and arrange for refreshments.

Demographics Team

Objectives

The Demographics Team is responsible for spying out the land. At the end of the training session, members of the team should be able to:

- Identify resources for demographic data.
- Gather demographic data on specific areas.
- Define potential target markets.
- Determine how the church can serve the target markets.
- Prepare the information needed by those who will doing visitations.

Identifying Resources

Resources for demographic data are:

- Chamber of Commerce
- Mapping software, e.g., Kingdom Combine
- Christian organizations, e.g., North American Mission Board

Gathering Data

The data should include:

- Population: Race, gender, marital status, age, income and occupation
- Who is a member of the church and who is not
- Statistics on affluent and poor areas (The church needs the financial support of the rich to meet the needs of the poor.)

Defining the Target Market

The target market is the group the church can serve based on your current ministries. The key question is: Who can we best serve?

Examples of target groups are:

- Seniors
- Youth
- Couples
- Children

Preparing to Go Out

The Demographic Team develops a plan for the church to minister to the needs of the people in the target market. The key questions are:

- What do we need to do to reach our target market?
- When we reach them, what do we need to meet their needs?

The team is also responsible for providing maps for the Tribal Leaders to use when conducting a blitz.

Prayer Leaders and Intercessors

Objectives

The entire Joshua Ministry strategy should be covered in prayer at all times. I recommend having a Prayer Leader in each ministry that will be partnering with the Evangelism Ministry in this effort. If your church is using the Fulfillment Hour model, each class will have a Prayer Leader. Intercessors from the Prayer Ministry and Prayer Leaders from the other ministries should join together to pray for the area and the people where you will be witnessing.

The objective of the training is for Prayer Leaders and Intercessors to:

- Pray effectively over the target area and the church.
- Enlist other congregants to pray, especially their Sunday School or Fulfillment Hour class members.

Approaching God

In order to approach God's throne with the confidence that our prayers will be heard and answered, we must:

- Confess any sin in our lives and seek repentance.
- Offer prayers of praise, adoration and thanksgiving.
- Pray for God to remove any hindering spirit within us.
- Pray based on God's Word.

Praying for the Event

Follow these guidelines when praying prior to the evangelism efforts:

- Get a map of the target area from the Demographic Team and/or names of family members, co-workers, friends, and neighbors.
- Pray and fast for the Holy Spirit to destroy hindering spirits in the atmosphere and to break strongholds in residents' lives.
- Pray that God will raise up laborers.
- Pray for the efforts of the ministries and Sunday School (Fulfillment Hour classes.
- Pray for lost persons. Ask that their hearts be opened and the enemy bound from them.
- Pray that Christ is formed in those who receive Christ (Galatians 4:19).
- Pray for any needs that they may have.
- Pray and intercede over the "Set the Captives Free" request forms.

Enlisting Others

The best way to involve others is by hosting a prayer-focused event or providing specific directions for their prayer time. Examples are:

- Prayer breakfast
- Prayer walks around the target area
- Bookmarks with prayer schedules printed on them

Tribal Leaders

Objectives	The Tribal Leaders are members of the Evangelism Ministry. They are responsible for leading the congregants in outreach efforts that are implemented through the Sunday School (Fulfillment Hour). Upon completion of the training, the Tribal Leaders will be able to:

- Act as liaison between the Evangelism Ministry and the Sunday School classes or Fulfillment Hour Outreach Leaders.
- Assist the Sunday School teacher or Fulfillment Hour Outreach Leader in coordinating evangelism activities, e.g., blitzes, Seed Casting, etc.
- Teach the Soul-Winning Evangelism Workshop.
- Prepare and direct blitzes, Seed Casting or personal visitation.
- Properly document results of all evangelism activities.
- Refer Sunday School teachers or Fulfillment Hour Outreach and Assimilation Leaders to ministries within the church and local organizations to assist them in meeting the needs of the people they meet during the evangelism activities.

Acting as Liaison

The Tribal Leaders are the first point of contact for the Sunday School teachers or Fulfillment Hour Outreach Leaders. It is important for the Tribal Leader to be sensitive to their needs and knowledgeable of:

- The Joshua Ministry strategy.
- The church's procedures for responding to ministry and missions needs.

Preparing for Visitations

Prior to the blitz or Seed Casting visitations, you should:

- Review the map and scout the neighborhood prior to the visitation.
- Assemble the materials for each team. These include:
  - Maps (from the Demographics Team)
  - Tracts
  - Door hangers
  - Clipboards,
  - Witnessing logs
  - Pens
  - Gift Bibles (Leave in vehicles until needed.)
- Obtain a list of resources in the church and community to assist in meeting people's needs.
- Obtain refreshments, if they will be provided.

NOTE: Use a highlighter to mark the specific streets or buildings each team will visit.

Tribal Leaders (cont'd)

Witnessing Maps

The Demographics Team will provide maps of the target area. The Tribal Leader should make sure there are enough copies for each group. The Tribal Leader assigns a different building, street or range of house numbers to each team so the burden is lessened and the group is able to complete the visitations within the scheduled time. Below are examples of how the maps should be marked to indicate the team assignments.

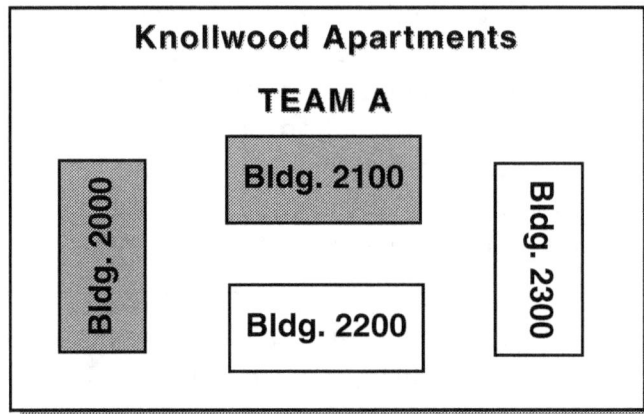

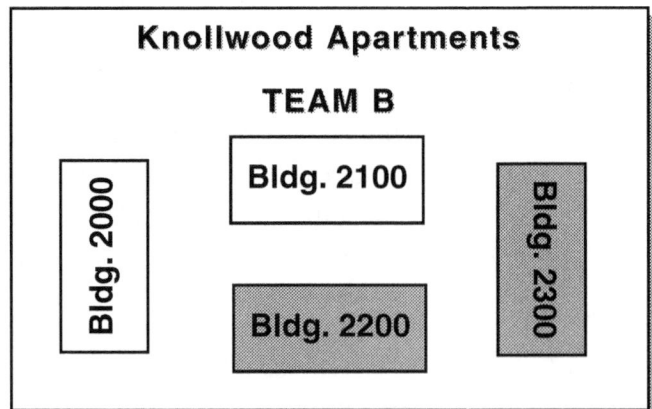

Knollwood Apartments

TEAM A

Bldg. 2000

Bldg. 2100

Bldg. 2200

Bldg. 2300

Knollwood Apartments

TEAM B

Bldg. 2000

Bldg. 2100

Bldg. 2200

Bldg. 2300

Tribal Leaders (cont'd)

Conducting Visitations

The Tribal Leader facilitates the entire event. The participants will look to the Tribal Leader for guidance and directions. The leader should:

- Arrive early to set up the room and refreshments, if provided.
- Greet the participants warmly when they arrive. Convey excitement about their presence and what God is about to do in people's lives.
- Facilitate the Soul-Winning Evangelism Workshop.
- Remind everyone of the do's and don'ts of witnessing:
  - Do be cordial.
  - Do respect people's time, circumstances and decisions.
  - Do not pressure anyone.
- Organize the group into teams following these guidelines:
  - Form groups of three (one to witness, one to pray and one to write).
  - Never send allow anyone to go alone. Always have at least two people in each team.
  - Do not send women by themselves. Try to have one man in each group.
  - Team new people with experienced people.
  - The Tribal Leader should be on a team. It is a good opportunity to model the process for first-time participants and help alleviate their fears.
- Make sure everyone knows how to properly complete the witnessing log.
- Review directions to the locations.
- Provide instructions so everyone is clear on where they are to go, what they are to do and when they should return.
- Lead the group in prayer before departing.

NOTE: It is best to have first-time participants arrive two hours early for the Soul-Winning Evangelism Workshop. Experienced participants should arrive at least thirty minutes prior to departure so they are present when the groups are formed.

Debriefing the Event

Immediately following the event, everyone returns to a central location to share testimonies on their experiences. This is a time to report results, praise God for the harvest and pray over needs that were discovered. Be sure to:

- Give God the glory for everything that was done.
- Allow each team an opportunity to share highlights of their experience.
- Provide guidance to assist in meeting any needs that were discovered.
- Pray.
  - Thank God for the results.
  - Ask God to protect the new converts.
  - Ask God's help in meeting people's needs.
- Review the witnessing logs to make sure they were completely properly.
- Complete the Evangelism Report to submit to the Communication Team.
- Give copies of the Witnessing Logs to the Follow-Up Team.

Outreach Leaders

Objectives

The Outreach Leader's job is to get people to carry out the evangelism tactic. The Fulfillment Hour model includes an Outreach Leader in each class. I recommend each of the church's ministries has an Outreach Leader.

The training objectives are to:

- Familiarize the Outreach Leaders with the process for the specific Joshua Ministry tactic you are implementing.
- Provide the Outreach Leaders a supply of "Set the Captives Free" request forms.
- Make sure the Outreach Leaders know what resources they have within the church and community to aid in meeting the needs of the people in the community.

Leading Others

The Outreach Leaders lead their ministry members and Sunday School (Fulfillment Hour) class members in evangelism efforts by:

- Communicating information to their ministries or classes about ongoing evangelism activities.
- Providing their class members the "Set the Captives Free" request forms and explaining how to use them.
- Encouraging their class members to fill out the "Set the Captives Free" request forms.
- Turning in the completed forms to the Prayer Ministry.
- Going with their class members to do evangelism and ministry in members' neighborhoods or on personal visitations.
- Distributing follow-up information to the appropriate person(s) or agency.

Assimilation Leaders

Objectives

In the Fulfillment Hour model, the Assimilation Leader helps new converts become a part of the Fulfillment Hour classes. The Assimilation Leader could be a worker from your New Members Ministry or anyone who is designated to follow-up with new converts.

The objective of the training is to:

- Equip the Assimilation Leaders to successfully interact with new converts.
- Provide information about your church's process so the Assimilation Leaders can answer questions and provide guidance.
- Familiarize the Assimilation Leaders with the process for referring people to other churches.

Welcoming Others

The Assimilation Leaders are to:

- Call the new converts, invite them to church and welcome them to into the family of God.
- Provide information about the church and answer questions.
- Contact the Evangelism Ministry's Follow-Up Team if assistance is needed locating resources to meet the convert's needs.

NOTE: Each Sunday, an Assimilation Leader should be assigned to greet people who join the church and get their contact information to follow-up with them later.

Follow-Up Team

Objectives

The Follow-Up Team is comprised of at least one person in your Evangelism Ministry. They are responsible for making or leading others in making direct contact with:

- People who have been evangelized.
- Non-active members.
- Visitors.

The Follow-Up Team are experts at getting people the help they need. The objective of their training is to ensure they are thoroughly knowledgeable of:

- The proper way to handle a contact with a prospect or new convert.
- Church and community resources.
- Church guidelines and process for meeting ministry and missions needs.

Identifying Resources

I suggest preparing a manual that lists contact information, available services and guidelines for referring people to:

- Ministries within your church.
- Ministries in other churches and para-church ministries in your local area.
- All government agencies in the area.

Someone on the team must be designated to update this information regularly. A binder works best so individual pages can be replaced as needed.

Contacting People Who Were Evangelized

Using the names on the Witnessing Logs, the Follow-Up Team will make sure:

- A personal visit or phone call is made to the people who were ministered to during the evangelism effort.
- People's needs are taken care of through your church's ministry, other churches, para-church groups or local agencies.
- A church has been suggested and contacted for those who chose not to attend your church. It is important the contact information is passed on to a local church in the area.

Contacting Non-Active Members

Sometimes a phone call to a non-active member is all that is needed to draw a person back into the flock. When contacting members who have been absent from the church for awhile, try to ascertain the following:

- Are there needs to be addressed?
- Are they attending another church?
- Were they wounded by your church? If so, help heal the situation.
- Do you need to do additional ministry?
- Can you refer them to another church? If they feel your church is not the place for them, then help them find a church.

Follow-Up Team (cont'd)

Contacting Visitors

Make visitors feel welcome and special by giving them individual attention. It is most effective to contact visitors immediately following the worship service. Two tactics that work well are:

- Distribute a visitors' package with information about your church's ministries
- Host a visitors' reception immediately following worship. Provide light refreshments and the visitors' packages.
- Hand deliver a visitors' package to their homes.

Communication Team

Objectives

The Communication Team is responsible for communicating the evangelism strategy to the church leadership and congregation. Their mission is to inform and promote. Their task is to keep the entire church aware and excited about outreach activities and results.

The objective of their training is to:

- Identify available media resources.
- Inform them of standard reports that they must provide on a regular basis, e.g., a weekly report to the pastor.
- Define the parameters they must operate within (do's and don'ts).

Promoting Events

Every available media source should be used to promote your evangelism efforts in the church and the target area. Be sure to take advantage of free public service announcements with local radio, television and newspapers.

Media sources to consider are:

- Church bulletin
- Church newsletter (yours and other churches)
- Community newspapers or newsletters (Apartment complexes often send newsletters or bulletins to their residents.)
- Evangelism bulletin board
- PowerPoint slide shows
- Posters
- Fliers
- Brochures
- Church website
- E-mail
- Direct mail (postcards or letters)

Publishing Results

It is vital that the church recognizes the work God is doing through them. Publishing the results of the evangelism efforts will give glory to God and generate excitement.

After each event, share the results with the pastor and congregation. The information should objectively reflect the effectiveness of the effort and the level of support shown by the church. Your published results might include:

- The number of people who were reached
- The number of people who received Christ
- The number of church members who participated
- Total attendance

Special Forces

Objectives

Special Forces is a group that helps their church and others to plant new churches. They operate like a military tactical unit, going to the enemy's front line to evangelize. Special Forces go to the places where Satan most frequently lures the lost—night clubs, liquor stores, malls, etc.

In addition to the Soul-Winning Evangelism Workshop, this group receives specialized training to develop one's spiritual life and prepare for spiritual warfare. Special attention is given to:

- Personal spiritual life, prayer and God's Word
- Spiritual warfare
- The authority of the believer
- The gifts of the Holy Spirit
- The work of the Holy Spirit

Special Forces members are part of a specialized unit in God's army. Those who desire to be apart of this team need to be fearless.

Executing the Mission

Members are never told what their assignment is until they report for service. This is so the enemy is not alerted to your coming. The team receives their assignment, moves in and strikes. Then, we catch people off guard and saturate them with our presence, love and message.

Soul-Winning Evangelism Workshop

Introduction

The Joshua Ministry's Soul-Winning Evangelism Workshop is designed to teach your congregants how to witness. It can be effectively used with small or large groups. At the end of this two-hour training, people who have never shared the gospel before are ready to witness to others immediately. Praise God!

The Soul-Winning Evangelism Workshop equips people to personal evangelism by placing five practical tools in their hands:

- The ability to love someone, regardless of their sins or their plight in life
- A personal testimony
- An invitation to attend your church
- Excitement
- Prayer

When combined with an evangelism blitz, this workshop is a powerful tool to liberate believers and win Souls for Christ. Knocking on doors is not the only method of evangelism, but door-to-door evangelism allows the participants to practice what they just learned and places them in front of people who have natural needs and a spiritual need for Christ. Comfort zones are broken, fear is broken, and the lost are saved.

Permission is granted to reproduce any part of this chapter.

Topics

This chapter contains the following topics:

Overview

Course Topics

The Soul-Winning Evangelism Workshop consists of seven lessons. Four of the lessons—The State of the Lost, The Word of God, The Holy Spirit in the Life of the Lost, and The Witness of the Believer—were taken from the book, *People Sharing Jesus* by Darrell W. Robinson. The lessons are:

- The State of the Unbeliever
- God's Word at Work in the Lost
- The Holy Spirit in the Life of the Lost
- The Holy Spirit in the Life of the Witness
- The Witness of the Believer
- Tools in Our Hands
- How to Share the Gospel

The State of the Unbeliever

How God Sees the Unbeliever

Once we know the unbeliever's state of being, it should motivate us to share Christ with them. Read the following Scriptures to understand God's view of the unbeliever.

1. Under sin (Romans 3:9)

2. Unrighteous (Romans 3:10)

3. Guilty before God (Romans 3:19)

4. Fallen short of God's glory (Romans 3:23)

5. Enemies of God (Romans 5:10)

6. Under a death sentence (Romans 6:23)

7. Spiritually dead to the things of God (I Corinthians 2:14–16)

8. Blinded by Satan (II Corinthians 4:3–4)

9. Dead in trespasses and sin; walking according to demonic influences; fulfilling the desires of the flesh and mind; children of wrath; having uncircumcised hearts; without Christ; aliens to the commonwealth of Israel; strangers to the covenants and promises of God; hopeless; and without God (Ephesians 2).

God's Word at Work in the Life of the Lost

The Power of God's Word

These are just a few Scriptures that indicate the importance of God's Word in the process of the new birth. God's Word cleanses us. His Word softens the hardened heart, allowing the Word to be received. Faith comes by hearing the Word. Once the Word is received, God's power is released and a spiritual birth takes place.

1. God's Word cleans (Psalm 119:9).

2. God's Word breaks up our hard heart (Jeremiah 23:29).

3. God's Word is like a sword (Ephesians 6:17).

4. God's Word builds faith for salvation (Romans 10:17, John 20:31).

5. God's Word is the power to save (Romans 1:16).

6. We are born again by God's Word (1:23).

We must be careful not to just invite people to church. God's Word has to be part of the process. If we do not use God's Word, there will be no cleansing, faith will not be released for salvation, the power of God will not be present to save, and a spiritual birth will not take place. The Scripture teaches us that God confirms His Word with signs following (Mark 16:20). Our results will only be minimal without prayer and God's Word.

The Holy Spirit in the Life of the Lost

The Holy Spirit at Work in the Lost

The Holy Spirit is at work in the life of the lost. Read the following Scriptures to see how the Holy Spirit:

1. Precedes the witness (Acts 9, 10).

2. He convicts the world of sin (John 16:8).

2. He reveals God's existence (Rom. 1:18–23).

The Holy Spirit in the Life of the Witness

The Holy Spirit at Work in Believers

The Holy Spirit prepares the witnesses by empowering them to share the gospel. He gives us words to say and places those with receptive hearts in our lives, so we can share Christ with them.

1. Enables the believer (Acts 1:8).

2. Gives him boldness (Acts 4:30–31).

3. Helps our inadequacies (Luke 12:12).

4. Creates divine appointments (John 4:1–30; Acts 8:30; Acts: 9:10–16).

I have seen confirmation of the work of the Holy Spirit in the many churches across the country that I have helped to implement the Joshua Ministry. The Holy Spirit gave boldness and power. He spoke through us, and brought people across our path who needed Christ. Each time, He brought us to a place where we knew it was nothing short of God's miraculous intervention and divine appointment.

The Witness of the Believer

God Needs Witnesses

God is Holy, powerful and sinless. Yet, He needs us to get the job done. As filthy as we are, God allows us to work with Him to win the lost.

In Acts 8, God knew what the Ethiopian eunuch was reading when He sent Philip to show him the way to salvation. In Acts 9, Jesus spoke directly to Paul, but did not tell him how to be saved. In Acts 10, an angel spoke to Cornelius, but the divine visitations never explained God's plan of salvation. God has given us the authority and responsibility to communicate the gospel to men (Matthew 10:1–15, 28:19; Mark 16:15). Without the witness of the believer, the message will never be shared. Moreover, it would only result in more people being bound for eternal damnation.

Read the following Scriptures to understand our need to witness:

1. The commission to witness is given to men (Matthew 28:19; Mark 16:15).

2. Men testified of what they had seen and heard (1 John 1:1–3).

3. The Ethiopian eunuch asked, "How can I, when there is no man guide me?" (Acts 8:30–31).

4. "Cornelius, a man will tell you what you should do" (Acts 10:1–6).

5. Paul said, "Lord, what would you have me do?" The Lord answered, "Arise and go into the city. A man will tell you what to do." (Acts 9:1–17).

Tools in Our Hands

Introduction

God gives us five practical tools to reach the lost:

- Love
- Personal testimony
- Invitation
- Excitement
- Prayer

When shared with others, these tools will be used by the Holy Spirit to win souls to Christ.

Love

Love draws the lost into God's kingdom. Communicating love enables people to experience God's love and acceptance, which opens the door for ministry.

There are two principles found in II Corinthians 5:17–19 that can be used to win the lost:

- **Do not condemn them for their sins.** We are to love them where they are, not condemn them to hell because of their sin.
- **God has given us the ministry of reconciliation**. Colossians 4:6 says, *"Let your speech be alway with grace, seasoned with salt, that ye may know how ye ought to answer every man."* That means we are not to put others down, but be gracious to bring out the best in others when we speak.

Personal Testimony

Your life story is called your testimony. People may argue with you about Scriptures, but they cannot dispute a strong testimony because it is factual.

Your testimony should consist of the following three points:

1. What your life was like before you received Christ
2. Your salvation experience
3. How your life has changed since you accepted Jesus

You should be able to share it in three minutes or less. Begin with the question, "May I share with you the most exciting thing that has ever happened in my life?" Then, end by asking, "Has anything like this ever happened to you?"

Use the form on the following page to write your testimony.

My Personal Testimony

Before Christ: _____
_____
_____
_____
_____
_____
_____
_____

My salvation experience: _____
_____
_____
_____
_____
_____
_____
_____

Since I accepted Jesus: _____
_____
_____
_____
_____
_____
_____
_____

Tools in Our Hands (cont'd)

Invitation

The kingdom of God is built on relationships. In John 4, after her encounter with Jesus, the woman at the well told the people in the village, "Come see a man!" Most people come to Jesus because someone invited them. We can begin by inviting people to attend church with us, but, at some point, we must share the gospel. I know we invite people to church to hear the salvation message, but what happens if they do not accept our invitation to church? The opportunity to share Christ may not come again.

Excitement

The woman at the well was so excited about her encounter with Jesus that she left her water pot. She ran back to the village and told the men, *"Come, see a man, which told me all things that ever I did: is not this the Christ? (John 4:29).* I believe these men knew her and they responded to her excitement. Many people will respond to the invitation based on our excitement.

Prayer

We can use prayer as a tool to open a door to share the gospel. In Acts 9:32–42, Peter prayed for two people. One was dead, and the other was sick. God raised one from the dead and healed the other. Prayer is one of our greatest tools. Sometimes the only thing we can do to meet a need is pray. Once we have prayed with a person for their needs, then we can share Christ. Jesus always met the natural need first. This gave Him the privilege to speak to the person's life.

How to Share the Gospel

The Gospel Message

When we share the gospel, the message should be inviting, giving hope and causing a response— even if it is negative. I tell the gospel story using Scriptures without citing chapter and verse, except Romans 10:9–10.

The gospel message should consist of five points:

1. **God's Purpose**
   a. God wants us to have a better life now (John 10:10).
   b. God also wants us to have an eternal life later (John 3:16).

2. **Our Sin Nature**
   a. Sin keeps us from what God has for us (Psalm 51:5).
   b. Adam's sin was passed on to all men (Romans 5:12).
   c. All have sinned (Romans 3:23).
   d. Sin must be judged (Romans 6:23).

3. **Repentance and Faith Alone**
   a. God commands all men to repent (Acts 17:30).
   b. Repent and be converted (Acts 3:19).
   c. We are saved by grace through faith, not by works (Ephesians 2:8–9).

4. **God's Plan**
   a. God came in the flesh in the person of Jesus (John 1:1, 14).
   b. Christ suffered for our sin (I Peter 3:18).
   c. God has laid our sin on Jesus (Isaiah 53:6).

5. **Surrender and Acceptance of Christ**
   a. God gives us the power to become His son or daughter (John 1:12).
   b. You must believe in your heart and confess with your mouth that Jesus is Lord of your life (Romans 10:9–10).
   c. We are to pray with the person to receive Christ. Our prayer includes:
      1. Acknowledgement of sin
      2. Asking God to forgive them of their sin
      3. An acceptance of Christ
   d. We unite ourselves with Christ through baptism (Romans 6:4).

How to Share the Gospel (cont'd)

Presenting the Gospel

The following is an example of how we can present the gospel when we go door-to-door.

Knock on the door.

Introduce yourself.

"My name is _____ , and I'm from _____ church. We are here to pray for any needs your family has."

Alternative: "We are here to meet our neighbors, share some information about our church, and assure you of your salvation.)

After listing their needs and praying with them, ask:

"If something were to happen to you today, where would you spend eternity?"

Alternatives:

"If you were to die, where would you spend eternity?"

"Do you ever think of spiritual things?"

"Have you ever accepted Jesus Christ as your personal savior?"

Any similar question is appropriate.

If their response is no, ask:

"May I take a few minutes to share God's plan of salvation? Mr./Ms. Prospect, God has a purpose for your life. He wants you to have an abundant life and eternal life. God's desire is for us to have a good life now, and to live with Him in eternity. However, we all have a sin nature that separates us from God. Because of that sin nature, we must repent and come to Christ by faith alone—nothing else. Then, we must accept what God has done through Jesus Christ, surrender our life and receive Christ by faith. Mr./Ms. Prospect, do you understand everything I said?"

If no, explain again.

Presenting the Gospel (cont'd)

If yes:

"Mr./Ms. Prospect, would you be willing to pray now to receive Jesus Christ?"

"No" indicates they are not ready to give up their current lifestyle or feel they need to correct something in their life. If the latter is the case, you must explain they will always be working on something that would hinder their surrendering to Christ. Christ wants us to come to Him so He can work out what we cannot. If they say they are willing to receive Christ, then say:

"I cannot save you. I can pray a prayer with you to receive Christ, but you have to mean the prayer from your heart."

Prayer:

"Heavenly Father, I heard good news today that Jesus Christ died for my sins. Father, I ask you to forgive me for all the sins in my life. I believe in my heart and confess with my mouth that Jesus died and rose from the grave for my sins. I accept Jesus right now as my Lord and my Savior. Lord Jesus, come into my heart. Please change my heart and my mind. Thank You for saving me. In Jesus' name, amen."

Rejoice with them!

Begin their assimilation into the family of God:

"You have a whole new family who are anxious to meet you. So you have a church in the area that you like to attend? Would you like me to pick you up for service?"

"I know you want to grow in your relationship with God. I suggest reading the Book of John because it will help you understand who Jesus is through His life and His works."

"I know you pray. Now that you have been reborn, you will want to spend more time in prayer, communing with God."

"God has given you the precious gift of eternal life. It is too good to keep to yourself. Let me teach you how to share this gift with others."

Get their name and contact information. Confirm spelling and all numbers.

Witnessing Tactics

Introduction　　God gives us unlimited ways of meeting people's needs and sharing the gospel. In this chapter, I will share some of the tactics that have been most effective in carrying out the Joshua Ministry strategies. This is not intended to be a comprehensive list, but instead ideas to springboard your creativity as you discern how God wants to use your church to minister to the people of your community.

Topics　　This chapter contains the following topics:

Adopt-a-Neighborhood

Description

The church(es) adopts a specific neighborhood as a missions project. Multiple churches or ministries can partner to meet the holistic needs of a community. By meeting the needs of your neighbors, you become the hands and feet of Christ and establish relationships that may lead to sharing the gospel.

An example of an Adopt-a-Neighborhood project is the Ministry of Hope started by my senior pastor's wife, Dr. Sadie T. McCalep. Dr. McCalep led the church to adopt the A. D. Williams Elementary School in Atlanta, Georgia. The ministry provides tutoring, annual clothing drives and toys at Christmas. This past Christmas, every fifth grader received a new bicycle for Christmas. The Ministry of Hope is committed to supporting the school and its families on an ongoing basis.

Goals

The goals of Adopt-a-Neighborhood are to:

- Plant seeds to harvest later.
- Build a bridge between the church and community.
- Give the church visibility in the community.
- Cause the community to become heralds who tell others what the church is doing to help them.

Implementation Steps

Follow these steps to implement Adopt-a-Neighborhood:

Step	Action
1	Select a neighborhood.
2	Pray over the area and the people.
3	Identify a need(s) you can address on a continual basis.
4	Determine what resources will be needed, including people, money, materials, legal permits, etc.
5	Plan your work and work your plan.
6	Promote participation in the church and community.
7	Record attendance and results. (See Tracking Results under Implementation Process).
8	Report results to the Communications Team and/or pastor.

Blitz

Description

A blitz is a concentrated effort to conduct group visitations in a specific area on a specific day. The blitz continues in a neighborhood until every household has either heard the gospel or received information, e.g., a tract. The group divides into teams that go door-to-door, sharing Christ and/or praying for the needs of those they visit.

Goals

The goals of a blitz are to:

- Invite people to church and/or share Christ in a group setting.
- Plant seeds to harvest later.
- Harvest those who are ready to accept Christ.
- Identify and meet needs of people in the community.
- Pray with people who have immediate needs.

Implementation Steps

Follow these steps to implement a blitz:

Step	Action
1	Have the Demographics Team spy the neighborhood.
2	Pray over the area and the people.
3	Train all participants in the Soul-Winning Evangelism Workshop. **NOTE:** See the Soul-Winning Evangelism Workshop under Training for a specific instructions of visitations.
4	Prepare to go out by gathering maps, tally forms, pens, clipboards, and Bibles. **NOTE:** Do not take Bibles door-to-door. They raise preconceived notions and reduce people's willingness to talk to you. Have Bibles in your vehicles for new converts who do not have their own. You can order affordable Bibles from the American Bible Society at www.bibles.com or 1-800-32-BIBLE.
5	Go. Divide into groups of no less than two people. I recommend three people in each group: one to witness, one to pray, and one to write.
6	Reconvene for the groups to share their testimonies of their experiences and to praise and thank God for the harvest.
7	Record attendance and results. (See Tracking Results under Implementation Process).
8	Report results to the Communications Team and/or pastor.

Blitz (cont'd)

Implementing Blitzes via Sunday School

The blitzes can be carried out by your Sunday School (Fulfillment Hour) classes. I recommend dividing the classes into tribes, and then sending the tribes out on a rotational basis. Tribal Leaders from the Evangelism Ministry coordinate each blitz. This provides an ongoing, systematic means of witnessing in your surrounding community.

Each class should have an Outreach Leader to encourage participation. After returning from the blitz, the Assimilation Leader contacts new converts and invites them to Sunday School (Fulfillment Hour) and worship. Once the new converts are enrolled in the class, the Discipleship Leader encourages them to grow spiritually and make other disciples.

Do's and Don'ts

You will create opportunities to plant seeds, if you are:

- Cordial.
- Respectful, especially of people's time and circumstances.
- Observant. Look for something that reveals their interest to use as an ice-breaker. Watch for immediate needs. Meet the need first, and then witness.

Being cordial, respectful and helpful will cause them to listen; if not now, then when you return later.

Brother-to-Brother

Description

Brother-to-Brother is an afternoon of fun and fellowship with thirty minutes of Bible instruction for middle and high school students. It is by far the most successfully compelling method to draw young people because the children tell other children, and it grows quickly.

After reading my book, *The Joshua Ministry: God's Witnessing Army,* Sheila Arnum, a member of Greenforest Community Baptist Church, decided to put the vision of the Joshua Ministry into action. Sheila organized Brother-to-Brother as a group of men who spend time with boys from high crime areas once a month, having fun and sharing God's Word.

The men are prosecutors, defense attorneys, ex-offenders, law enforcement officers, entrepreneurs, college students, teachers, foster parents, fathers of incarcerated men and boys, ministers and others. Their activities include go-carts, dunk tanks, volleyball, basketball, horse shoes, football, foosball, ping-pong, limbo stick, smoothie stand and more. At these monthly fellowships, the boys learn how to be men while they play, eat, sing, pray and study the Bible together.

The boys are transported by bus from their neighborhoods to the fellowship location. The men meet and fellowship with each other from noon until 1:00 PM. When the boys arrive at 1:00 PM, the men greet them with love as they exit the buses. The event lasts until 5:00 PM.

While Sheila's program is designed to reach at-risk boys who live in high crime areas, her concept can be used to effectively reach all middle school and high school students. You can call it whatever you like as long as it has the following components:

- Fellowship
- Fun
- Bible study (30 minutes maximum)

Bible instruction is a must. If you do not include Bible study, then the gathering is just another day of fun. The Bible is what separates this event from similar secular activities.

Goals

The primary goal of Brother-to-Brother (or any similar program) is to draw middle and high school students to Christ. Additional goals may be achieved by your specific program.

Brother-to-Brother (cont'd)

Implementation Steps

Follow these steps to implement a youth outreach program:

Step	Action
1	Select a neighborhood.
2	Pray over the area and the people.
3	Determine needed resources: space, adult volunteers, money, food, games, Bibles, etc. NOTE: Costs can be minimized by asking adults from the church to donate food items. If you are in a climate that gets cold during the winter months, find facilities for indoor activities. It is important the program does not shut down, but continues throughout the year.
4	Identify other community resources and government agencies to support your program.
5	Obtain legal permits, including parental consent and medical release forms, if necessary.
6	Invite middle and high school students in the neighborhood to a fellowship event. This is your bait. Make it fun!
7	Record attendance and results. (See Tracking Results under Implementation Process).
8	Report results to the Communications Team and/or pastor.

Crusade

Description

Crusades take the ministry of the church to the streets. A crusade may be held in a park or on a street corner. Examples are outdoor concerts and drama (plays) on the street. The event should include a sermonette, a short message of the gospel. Tracts and guest cards are distributed to the crowd.

Goals

The goals of a crusade are to:

- Share the gospel message and an invitation to accept Christ.
- Invite people to church.

Implementation Steps

Follow these steps to host a crusade:

Step	Action
1	Partner with other ministries in the church to take the gospel to the streets.
2	Pray to discern God's desire for the event. Also, pray for the people and the area.
3	Plan the event, identifying needed resources, e.g., equipment, materials, refreshments, etc.
4	Obtain legal permission from local officials.
5	Prepare forms to record the names and contact information of new converts.
6	Conduct the crusade.
7	Clean up the area afterward. Do not leave the site covered with trash.
8	Give the contact information for the new converts to the Follow-Up Team.
9	Record attendance and results. (See Tracking Results under Implementation Process).
10	Report results to the Communications Team and/or pastor.

Guest Cards

Description

A guest card is a small card, the size of a business card, that is used to invite people to worship, Sunday School (Fulfillment Hour) or an event. It is the most simplistic, user-friendly tool the entire congregation can use to invite people to church.

The card should include the following information:

- The name of the church
- The church's address and telephone number
- A phrase inviting them to be your be your guest
- Space for the church member's name and telephone number

It is not necessary to have the cards professionally printed. You can create very attractive cards on your computer and print them on perforated business cards, which can be purchased at any office supply store. Here is the card we use at my church.

Greenforest Community Baptist Church
3250 Rainbow Drive
Decatur, Georgia 30034
404.486.1120

Will you be my guest?

Worship Times: 7:00 a.m., 9:45 a.m., 12:00 p.m.
Fulfillment Hour: 8:35 a.m., 10:00 a.m., 11:30 a.m.

Name _____

Phone _____

Goal

The goal of the guest card is to get people to visit your worship service, Sunday School (Fulfillment Hour) or a specific event.

Implementation Steps

Follow these steps to implement guest cards:

Step	Action
1	Design and print your cards.
2	Place the cards in the pews or ask the ushers to distribute them during worship service.
3	Introduce the cards from the pulpit.
4	Instruct your congregants to: ■ Write their names and phone numbers on the cards so prospects can contact them. ■ Carry the cards with them in their wallets. ■ Give cards to family, neighbors, friends and co-workers.
5	Recognize visitors who came as a result of receiving a guest card. Make them feel special and welcome.

Multiplication By One

Description

Disciples not only win others, but also teach those they have won to do the same. In Multiplication By One, each member commits to win a person to Christ or invite someone to church weekly, monthly, or quarterly. If everyone wins one, and that one wins one, think how many will be won for Christ.

Paul teaches us to entrust to reliable men who will teach others.

> *"And the things that thou hast heard of me among many witnesses, the same commit thou to faithful men, who shall be able to teach others also."*
> *(2 Timothy 2:2)*

If every church member began participating in January, your membership would double by the end of the year.

Goal

The goal of Multiplication By One is for each member to win one person to Christ in one year.

Implementation Steps

Discipling others means getting involved in people's lives. It means meeting their needs, answering their questions, encouraging them and guiding them in their spiritual growth.

If new converts are to become disciples who make other disciples, you must teach them how to witness. Follow these steps when teaching others how to share Christ.

Step	Action
1	Each member commits to work with one new convert each year.
2	Accompany your new convert to the Soul-Winning Evangelism Workshop.
3	When making visitations to share Christ, allow them to watch you model the process.
4	Share the following do's and don'ts of visitations: ■ Don't pressure people. ■ Do be kind, caring, and demonstrate the love of Christ. ■ Do respect people's time and decision. NOTE: See the Soul-Winning Evangelism Workshop for instructions on visitations.
5	Teach them to properly complete the Witnessing Log.
6	Teach them to model the process to someone else.

Neighborhood Projects

Description

Neighborhood projects are one-time missions efforts to assist neighborhoods in meeting a specific need. Examples are:

- Building a playground
- Making minor repairs for senior citizens
- Planting a neighborhood garden
- Cleaning up the neighborhood

Goals

Neighborhood projects are designed to:

- Meet an immediate need in the community.
- Plant seeds for harvest.
- Create visibility for the church(es).
- Build a bridge between the church and community.

Implementation Steps

Follow these steps to implement a neighborhood project:

Step	Action
1	Select a neighborhood.
2	Pray over the area and the people.
3	Identify a need(s) you can address immediately.
4	Determine what resources will be needed, including people, money, materials, legal permits, etc.
5	Plan your work and work your plan.
6	Promote participation in the church and community.
7	Record attendance and results. (See Tracking Results under Implementation Process).
8	Report results to the Communications Team and/or pastor.

Seed Casting

Description

Church members go door-to-door in new subdivisions, inviting people to church or placing door hangers at the new residences. Participants knock on doors and invite people to attend worship. If no one answers, they leave a door hanger containing information about the church, e.g., location, worship times, ministries, etc.

Seed casting is a congregational strategy that works best when implemented through the Sunday School (Fulfillment Hour). The adult classes or tribes are assigned to go out on a rotational basis.

Goals

The goal of seed casting is to share information about the church with new residents and invite them to worship, Sunday School (Fulfillment Hour) or a specific event.

Implementation Steps

Follow these steps to seed casting:

Step	Action
1	Locate new construction in the surrounding community. NOTE: If your neighborhood does not have new construction, visit apartment complexes. They are likely to have turnover within a year.
2	Obtain door hangers.
3	Identify a need(s) you can address immediately.
4	Determine what resources will be needed, including people, money, materials, legal permits, etc.
5	Plan your work and work your plan.
6	Promote participation in the church and Sunday School (Fulfillment Hour).
7	Record attendance and results. (See Tracking Results under Implementation Process).
8	Report results to the Communications Team and/or pastor.

Set the Captives Free

Description

"Set the Captives Free" is a tactic whereby Sunday School (Fulfillment Hour) class members help each other "possess their land" by evangelizing their neighborhoods or making personal visitations to family members, friends, neighbors or co-workers. The program is based upon Luke 4:18–19.

> *The Spirit of the Lord is upon me, because he hath anointed me to preach the gospel to the poor; he hath sent me to heal the brokenhearted, to preach deliverance to the captives, and recovering of sight to the blind, to set at liberty them that are bruised, To preach the acceptable year of the Lord.*

Members identify the ten people with whom they want most to share Christ so the Prayer Ministry can pray for them. Members submit forms to the Prayer Ministry to request a neighborhood blitz or personal visitation. The Prayer Ministry prays until God gives release to go, and the class goes out together. The member who initiated the request disciples the new convert.

Goals

The goal of "Set the Captives Free" is to help Sunday School (Fulfillment Hour) class members take back their neighborhoods and share Christ with their loved ones.

Implementation Steps

Follow these steps to implement "Set the Captives Free":

Step	Action
1	Partner with your Prayer Ministry or a team of intercessors.
2	Establish a process for the Prayer Ministry to communicate requests to the Evangelism Ministry.
3	Create the request forms.
4	Pray for the Holy Spirit to awaken a passion for the lost in your church and to go before you when you witness.
5	Introduce the program to the Sunday School (Fulfillment Hour).
6	Introduce the program to the congregation from the pulpit.
7	Conduct the blitz or make the visitations. (See Soul Winning Workshop in the Training section for visitation instructions.)
8	Record results. (See Tracking Results under Implementation Process).
9	Report results to the Communications Team and/or pastor.

My 10 Most Wanted

1. _____
2. _____
3. _____
4. _____
5. _____
6. _____
7. _____
8. _____
9. _____
10. _____

SET THE CAPTIVES FREE!

I want to set the captives free!

Please help me take back my:
- ❑ Neighborhood
- ❑ Family, friend or neighbor

Name of Neighborhood: _____
Name of Person You Are Reclaiming:

_____

Relationship to You: _____

Your Name: _____
Address: _____ Apt./Unit: _____
City: _____ Zip: _____
Phone: _____
Your Fulfillment Hour Class:

_____

**Return the form to your Fulfillment Hour
Outreach Leader or Shepherd.**

Tract Distribution

Description

A tract is a leaflet that communicates the gospel message that Jesus died for our sins, rose again and gives the free gift of eternal life to those who accept Him as their personal Savior. Tracts are simplistic, user-friendly witnessing tools because:

- You only have to say, "Here's something to read in your spare time."
- They can be distributed anywhere.

Tracts are like business cards. They identify Christians. Therefore, we should never leave home without them.

> That which was from the beginning, which we have heard, which we have seen with our eyes, which we have looked upon, and our hands have handled, of the Word of life; (For the life was manifested, and we have seen it, and bear witness, and shew unto you that eternal life, which was with the Father, and was manifested unto us;) That which we have seen and heard declare we unto you, that ye also may have fellowship with us: and truly our fellowship is with the Father, and with his Son Jesus Christ (1 John 1:2).

Tracts may be obtained by:

- Ordering them from your denominational headquarters.
- Purchasing them from Christian bookstores.
- Designing your own.

Goals

The goal of tract distribution is to share the gospel with as many people as possible as we are going about our daily lives.

Implementation Steps

Follow these steps to implement tract distribution:

Step	Action
1	Obtain the tracts in bulk.
2	Distribute the tracts to the congregation and make it easy for them to secure more whenever needed.
3	Encourage your congregation to make witnessing part of their lifestyle of witnessing.

Administrative Forms

Introduction

This chapter contains the forms you will use to track the results of your evangelism efforts. You may reproduce the forms in this chapter.

Forms

This chapter contains the following forms:

Forms	Page
Witnessing Log	70
Evangelism Report	71

Witnessing Log

Tribe/Ministry: _____

Date: _____

No.	Street/Bldg.	House/Apt. #	Name (if provided)	Phone (if provided)	Left Tracts	Shared Christ	Received Salvation	Rededication	Assured Salvation	Prayed for Needs	Comments
1.											
2.											
3.											
4.											
5.											
6.											
7.											
8.											
9.											
10.											
11.											
12.											
13.											
14.											
15.											
16.											
17.											
18.											
19.											
20.											

Evangelism Report

Tribe/Ministry: _____ **Date:** _____

Type of Outreach: ❑ Blitz   ❑ Seed Casting   ❑ Personal Visitation

Item	Qty.
Shared Christ	_____
Received Christ	_____
Assured of Salvation	_____
Rededication	_____
Prayed for Needs	_____
Enrolled in Sunday School (Fulfillment Hour)	_____
Total Contacts	_____
First-Time Participants	_____
Total Participants	_____

Implementation Notes

Notes

Notes

Notes

Notes

Ask Rev. Hopewell to Help Your Church

Available Seminars

Soul-Winnning Workshop

Spiritual Warfare and Evangelism

Evangelism Through the Sunday School

Youth Evangelism Strategy

Men Reaching Men

Evangelism Styles

Evangelism Strategies

Cults and World Religions

The Holy Spirit and His Works

Keys to Becoming an Effective Associate Minister

How to Effectively Pray

Salvation Counseling

Rev. David Hopewell, Sr.
(404) 486-6728 • david.hopewell@greenforest.org

Reverend David Hopewell, Sr., D.Min. is Minister of Evangelism at Greenforest Community Baptist Church in Decatur, Georgia and is the founder of the Joshua Ministry. For over twenty-five years, Rev. Hopewell has helped pastors in the areas of leadership development, church growth and evangelism. He has served as an associate pastor for over twenty years. He also helped to plant five churches, two of which he pastored.

Rev. Hopewell has a passion for the lost and an even greater passion for equipping the body of Christ to reach the lost. He is a evangelism strategist, motivational speaker and seminar leader. His wife and four children assist him in ministry.

If you have questions regarding the Joshua Ministry or would like to schedule a seminar or speaking engagement, you may contact Rev. Hopewell at (404) 486-6728 or david.hopewell@greenforest.org.

The Joshua Ministry
www.joshuaministry.net